£9.99

D0334366

PART-TIME WORKERS

Anna Allan studied sociology and personnel management at Bath University, followed by a masters degree in organisational behaviour from the University of London. She has worked as an HR manager for 20 years, mostly in the financial services industry and has long been an active campaigner for 'people-friendly' employment practices. She is a trustee of the charity New Ways to Work – which campaigns for alternative work patterns – and author of two information packs on Flexible Working and Carer Leave. A Fellow of the IPD, Anna regularly contributes to the activities of her local branch.

Lucy Daniels is a work/life consultant specialising in flexible working practices and family-friendly employment policies, on which she has written extensively. She is a founder and former director of the national charity Parents at Work, where she initiated the annual Employer of the Year Awards. More recently, she helped to set up and launch the UK branch of international providers of corporate work/life services, Ceridian Performance Partners (formerly known as WFD). Publications include a recently launched Childcare Information Pack for employers, sponsored by the DfEE, and a recently launched Employers' Childcare Information Pack.

000163614

The Institute of Personnel and Development is the leading publisher of books and reports for personnel and training professionals, students, and all those concerned with the effective management and development of people at work. For details of all our titles, please contact the Publishing Department:

tel 020 8263 3387

fax 020 8263 3850

e-mail publish@ipd.co.uk

The catalogue of all IPD titles can be viewed on the IPD website:

www.ipd.co.uk

PART-TIME WORKERS

ANNA ALLAN
AND
LUCY DANIELS

INSTITUTE OF PERSONNEL AND DEVELOPMENT

Dedicated to Jill Dawson

Design and typesetting by
Wyvern 21, Bristol

Printed in Great Britain by
the Short Run Press, Exeter

British Library Cataloguing-in-Publication Data
A catalogue record for this book is available
from the British Library

ISBN 0-85292-813-0

NB Throughout this publication the male gender has,
in general, been used for convenience, but it should
be read to include the female gender.

INSTITUTE OF PERSONNEL
AND DEVELOPMENT

IPD House, Camp Road, Wimbledon, London SW19 4UX
Tel: 020 8971-9000   Fax: 020 8263-3333
Registered office as above. Registered Charity No. 1038333
A company limited by guarantee. Registered in England No. 2931892

Contents

Acknowledgements

We would like to thank everyone who helped us in putting this book together, in particular Clare Genis, Pam Walton and our editor, Richard Goff.

Other titles in the series

Bullying and Sexual Harassment
Tina Stephens

Creating a Staff Handbook
Clare Hogg

Drugs and Alcohol Policies
Tricia Jackson

Induction
Alan Fowler

Smoking Policies
Tricia Jackson

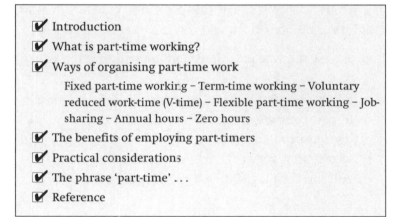

What is part-time working?

Introduction

The increase in part-time working has been a major feature of employment trends over the past decade, and forecasts show the growth continuing. The benefits of part-time working go two ways: by employing part-time workers, an enterprise can schedule its operations to match customer needs while remaining competitive in controlling staff costs. Offering opportunities for part-time working may also be a valuable aid to recruiting and retaining skilled workers. Employees may value the opportunity to combine part-time work with other aspects of life, such as caring for other family members, study, wind-down to retirement or community involvement.

Although there are advantages to new ways of working for both employer and employee, you may need to adopt new ways of supervising work to get the best from the arrangement for everyone concerned. In many cases, having a formal policy or clear guidelines may enhance the status of part-timers, underlining their value to the organisation as a whole. The purpose of this book is to enable you as an employer or manager to:

- review the way part-time staff are employed in your business
- adjust your policies and practices to make better use of part-time working for the benefit of the organisation and your staff
- ensure that your practices are in line with new employment legislation as of the year 2000.

What is part-time working?

The new European Union (EU) Part-Time Workers Directive, which will be adopted into UK legislation in the year 2000, defines a part-time worker as:

> anyone who works fewer hours than a comparable full-time worker at the same establishment.

Historically, opinions on what is 'part-time' have varied. The UK government, for example, chooses to classify part-time work as anything under 30 hours a week. Originally introduced in the 1950s as a way to overcome staffing shortages by encouraging married women back to work, part-time working has gradually become a significant part of many employers' staffing strategies as the need for flexibility and responsiveness to customer demands has grown. Although traditional part-time working simply meant fewer hours a day or fewer days a week within the standard full-time format, over the years it has developed to encompass a variety of formats, which can be summarised thus:

simple fixed part-time working

term-time working

voluntary reduced work time (V-time)

flexible part-time working

job-share

annual hours

complex zero hours

These are considered in turn below.

Ways of organising part-time work

Part-time working can be organised in a number of ways to suit the demands of your business and the needs of your employees. In this section we shall be explaining the options, who uses them and the practical considerations you should take into account when selecting a part-time working option.

Fixed part-time working

What is it?

This is 'traditional' part-time working. An employee works a reduced number of hours a day, or fewer days a week, or perhaps a regular pattern of alternate weeks.

3

Angela had only recently qualified as a chartered surveyor when she found herself pregnant with her first child. Because her husband was also in a professional job with long hours, she decided to switch to part-time working on returning from maternity leave. She now works three days a week, spending the remaining two with her young son.

Who uses it and why?

Traditional part-time work is both liked and widespread because it is the simplest system to administer and to understand. Typically, organisations tend to restrict it to clerical (or sometimes secretarial) work. Other examples of traditional part-time workers are cleaners and care assistants.

Practical considerations

Many organisations are increasingly finding traditional part-time arrangements too rigid to accommodate the fluctuating staffing levels demanded by their business.

Term-time working

What is it?

This system was designed to appeal to parents of school-age children; an employee works only during school terms – sometimes working reduced hours to accommodate the school day. The employee is paid only for hours worked and may enjoy pro rata benefits.

Who uses it and why?

Again, this is a fairly straightforward arrangement often used to retain more senior female employees (such as supervisors or departmental managers) once they have had children. It can be a powerful recruitment tool for attracting such workers where full-time staff are unavailable, and has proved popular with local government and some retailers. Recent figures suggest that around 4.2 per cent of all employees work on a term-time basis.

Practical considerations

Not all jobs can be worked on a term-time-only basis. Where continuity of cover is required it may be possible to 'fill the gap' by other means (see the case-study below). Furthermore, communication can become a problem during the long summer holiday; in some businesses, also, six to eight weeks is too long a time to be away.

> Margaret works as a section supervisor in a large supermarket. She has a term-time-only contract, which allows her to look after her children during their school holidays. When she is not at work, her place is taken by Simon – a degree student planning a career in retail management and currently available for work only during holiday periods.

Voluntary reduced work-time (V-time)

What is it?

A V-time scheme allows an employee voluntarily to trade income for time off for a limited period. Typically, he is allowed to reduce his working time by anything from 5 to 50 per cent for up to a year while remaining in the same job and with a right to return to full-time working at the end of the period. The working-time reduction can be in the form of a shorter working day or week, or a block of time off during the year.

Who uses it and why?

V-time schemes have been around in the USA since 1976 but have so far not proved popular in the UK. They can be powerful retention tools where skilled staff find themselves having to cope with outside responsibilities that might otherwise lead them to resign from a full-time job.

> Malcolm was working as a full-time departmental manager when his elderly but sprightly mother broke her hip. He discussed the matter with his brother and sister; all three decided that they would prefer to nurse their mother at home rather than put her into care. Because Malcolm's employer ran a V-time scheme, Malcolm was able to agree a 20 per cent reduction in his working week (to four days) for a six-month period. By the end of that period his mother had recovered sufficiently to allow Malcolm to return to full-time work.

Practical considerations

V-time schemes can be more easily managed in larger organisations. If a number of people are working reduced hours, the saved time can be 'pooled' to make another job and a new employee hired. In a smaller business where one employee is working reduced hours, the burden of making up the work is likely to fall on other staff as overtime.

Flexible part-time working

What is it?

As with fixed part-time working, here the employee has a contract for a guaranteed number of hours a week. In addition, however, he may be required to work extra hours to accommodate peaks in activity.

Who uses it and why?
It has become popular with retailers attempting to reduce employment costs. Additional hours worked by part-timers need not attract premium overtime rates until they have worked the same number of hours as full-timers. (It is important that this is clearly stated in the employment contract to avoid any subsequent misunderstandings.)

Practical considerations
The major disadvantage is that this system sometimes requires greater flexibility from employees than they are able to offer – particularly where they have commitments (such as childcare or eldercare) pushing them to work part-time in the first place. One retailer, Asda, has attempted to overcome this problem by allowing staff to swap shifts with colleagues, enabling them to balance flexibility at work with out-of-work responsibilities.

Job-sharing

What is it?
Typically, two people share one full-time job, each doing half the work and receiving half the pay, holidays and benefits. The most common arrangement is for each sharer to work two-and-a-half days a week, but sharers may also work mornings or afternoons or alternate weeks. Job-shares have grown in number since the early 1980s. According to the autumn 1997 *Labour Force Survey*, some 177,000 employees (0.8 per cent of all employees) were working in job-shares, 89 per cent of whom were women. It has become especially popular in local government: a 1994 survey carried out by

New Ways to Work found that 62 per cent of the 249 local authorities surveyed had a formal job-share scheme, while more than half the remainder had informal arrangements.

> Barbara and Richard are both managers with a clearing bank. They currently share the job of equal opportunities manager, which enables each to work two-and-a-half days a week and so to spend more time with their young families. The bank has retained two skilled managers and a key job, into which a full-time employee may be promoted at some future date.

Who uses it and why?

Job-sharing is typically viewed as a more appropriate way of enabling two skilled professionals to work less than full-time. Employers benefit from two different sets of skills and experience and, where a job is essential to the organisation, it ensures the survival of the post in its full-time format. Job-sharing can be used both as a recruitment and a retention tool, and may be a more attractive option to men, because it retains the notion of managerial status.

Practical considerations

Good communication between sharers is essential; most arrange some sort of regular hand-over of information. It helps if the two people planning to share know each other beforehand, and it is important that they can work well together and with other colleagues. There are a number of practical considerations to take into account in order to get the best out of a new job-share. A simpler alternative to job-sharing is *job-splitting*, where the tasks within a single job are grouped into two independent part-time jobs. More information on job-sharing and job-splitting can be found in Chapters 4 and 6.

Annual hours

What is it?

In such schemes as th:s the time an employee is contracted to work is defined over the whole year rather than by the week. Hours worked are not spread evenly but scheduled to accommodate peaks and troughs in business activity. Typically, the contract specifies exactly when the majority of hours are to be worked, but a portion of contractual hours is held in reserve to be worked as business demands. An employee can be contracted to work both full-time or part-time under an annual hours scheme. Around 4.5 per cent of the workforce is employed on such schemes.

> Annette is a consultant to the financial services industry, with specialist accounting skills. She agreed with her employer that she would work for a minimum of 50 days each year, working more if required and if her other commitments allowed her to do so. She ended up working more days but, by working only when it was convenient, she was still able to balance work with bringing up her two young daughters. For Annette, the advantage of her annual hours arrangement is that she knows she will receive a guaranteed minimum level of income every month.

Who uses it and why?

Annual hours schemes have been around since the 1950s – initially in continuous process industries. The last few years have seen a dramatic surge in their popularity with organisations as diverse as major retailers and ITN employing staff on annual hours contracts.

Practical considerations

A major drawback is that these schemes can be complex and hence difficult for staff to understand. Many schemes pay salaries in equal instalments, so there may be periods of the year when an employee 'owes' the employer a certain number of hours. It is important to have a clause in the employment contract enabling you (as the employer) to recover payments should staff leave before working the hours in credit. Unless annual hours are genuinely appropriate for your business, it may be better to opt for a simpler form of part-time working.

Zero hours

What is it?

An individual is contracted to be available for work – usually within specified periods such as 'Monday to Friday' or 'Saturday only' – with no guarantee that any work will be forthcoming.

Who uses it and why?

A number of retailers have experimented with zero hours, as have some health authorities attempting to schedule nursing cover. In theory, zero hours contracts provide a reserve army of labour available at short notice but without the cost of recruiting temporary staff. Employees involved are likely to be those who were previously employed by the business on another contract but who are no longer able to commit themselves to regular hours because of family circumstances or other commitments (such as studying).

Practical considerations

Zero hours contracts do not always live up to their promise, because reserve employees may inevitably be unavailable to work when needed precisely because of the circumstances that forced them to take on such a contract in the first place.

In addition, the interpretation of zero hours contracts under employment law is very complex. An employer might be misled into thinking that continuity of employment does not exist, whereas in practice it often does. The employer could then find himself responsible for the provision of all those benefits to which employees may become entitled, such as holiday pay and maternity leave and pay. He could also be open to a claim of unfair dismissal if he decides to end the relationship with his zero hours workers. We do not recommend the use of these contracts without qualified legal advice.

The benefits of employing part-timers

When managers are asked to list the benefits of employing part-time staff, the most frequently cited responses are these:

- The labour supply can be tailored to trading peaks, reducing underemployment during quiet times and making the business more competitive.
- Offering part-time work provides a larger potential pool from which to recruit.
- Staff with specialist skills can be employed for the limited number of hours when these skills are needed.

A respondent to an Institute of Management survey expressed the benefits of part-time workers this way[1]:

Quality people who are available to work part-time are more valuable than less experienced or skilled people who can work full-time.

In addition, an employer may be able to enjoy the following benefits:

- Overtime costs are reduced. There is no legal requirement to pay part-timers premium rates for overtime until they have worked the same number of hours as full-timers, so asking part-timers to work extra hours can minimise overtime costs.
- Less space may be needed, representing a reduction in overhead costs.
- Staff employed for a very small number of hours may have earnings that fall below the National Insurance (NI) threshold, representing a saving to both employer and employee.

Practical considerations

- Communication difficulties can increase – but we shall be discussing this in later chapters.
- Part-timers are sometimes perceived to be less committed, less loyal and less motivated. However, this appears to be a function of how well they are treated *vis-à-vis* full-timers.
- There is a risk that work quality may suffer if no hand-over periods are built into working time.
- Part-time working may not provide the flexibility you are looking for if employees have other commitments pushing them into working part-time.
- In the early days, the management of part-timers can

require more time than that of full-timers until the organisation adapts to this new way of working.

- Depending on the type of part-time system operated, administration can be more complex. Computer software packages can help to redress this, and are covered in Chapter 6.
- Many organisations have traditionally offered a lesser package of benefits to part-time staff, with the result that they were seen as a cheaper resourcing option. This strategy is becoming increasingly risky, because it can be perceived as indirectly discriminating against women and may also fall foul of the new Part-Time Workers Directive. The legal implications will be considered in Chapter 2.

The phrase 'part-time' . . .

The widespread adoption of a long-hours culture by UK organisations has led to the derogatory use of the term 'part-timer' to imply someone who is not making a full contribution to the employing organisation. Although this attitude is not reflected in managers' opinions of part-time workers, many organisations have substituted such terms as 'key-time worker' for 'part-timer' to emphasise the contribution made by such employees.

Reference

1 HASTINGS M. *Flexibility and Fairness: A survey of managers' attitudes to part-time employment and part-time employees.* London, Institute of Management, 1996.

Why do I need a policy on part-time working?

Whatever the size and scope of your enterprise, you will benefit from having a clear policy on the role of part-time working in your organisation. There are three advantages in particular:

1 Part-time working makes good business sense.
2 A clear policy on part-time working will both encourage diversity in your workforce and minimise the risk of contravening legislation relating to discrimination.
3 You will be prepared for the EU Part-Time Workers Directive when it comes into force in the year 2000.

Part-time working makes good business sense

Many organisations are already convinced by the sound business arguments for employing part-time workers. For example, a recent IMC/Manpower plc report looking at corporate employment strategies and trends revealed that 63 per cent of companies use part-time workers, while 33 per cent have job-sharers[1]. The overwhelming reason for choosing such working methods – cited by over 70 per cent of respondents – is customer demand for longer hours of operation. Furthermore, 30 per cent of respondents said they would be increasing part-time working over the following 12 months, while 19 per cent planned to increase job-sharing. According to *Labour Force Survey* figures, over 6.5 million people – nearly 25 per cent of the workforce – are already working part-time[2]. As the authors of a guide to flexible working state[3]:

> Some organisations need to be open for longer than the traditional full-time working week [*of up to 40 hours*]. In many organisations with longer opening hours it is no longer possible for one person to be available throughout the working week. This questions the whole concept of full-time and part-time. Full-time no longer coincides with traditional opening hours. This is increasingly common in retail organisations. Here, employing two part-time employees or two job-sharers can be a practical way of covering the week.

As we have already seen, employing part-time staff can enable you to tailor your labour supply to trading peaks, reducing underemployment during quiet times and making the business more competitive. In addition, unless your contract of employment specifically states otherwise, there is no legal requirement to pay part-timers premium rates for overtime until they have worked the same number of hours as full-timers, so asking part-timers to work extra hours can minimise overtime costs.

Where staff are employed for a very small number of hours they may have earnings below the NI threshold, representing a saving to both the employer and employee. And employing staff with specialist skills only for the small number of hours they may be needed can enable you to make best use of your financial resources.

Offering part-time work can provide a larger potential pool from which to recruit – *Labour Force Survey* figures show that 86.6 per cent of those working part-time do not want to work full-time. In addition, 85 per cent of the predicted 1.5 million increase in the workforce over the next 10 years will be female. Because many women work part-time by choice, you will be able to attract more of this potential workforce. Even among men there is a small but noticeable trend towards choosing part-time work, and one million are now employed on this basis. Expanding your recruitment pool is particularly important if you are operating in an area where there are skills shortages or fierce competition for staff.

Offering part-time work may also enable you to retain highly skilled and long-serving members of staff who would otherwise be forced to leave your employment because of changes in their own circumstances. One of the summary recommendations of a select committee on part-time working warned that[4]:

The barriers to voluntary part-time and flexible working at senior levels in organisations and in professional jobs may be a waste of expensively acquired skills in both the public and private sectors. We urge employers and government departments to examine their employment practices to see whether . . . there are opportunities for job sharing, how greater status could be accorded to part-time work and how to ensure that employees working part-time are still able to secure their career development and to be considered equally for promotion.

The opportunity to work part-time is likely to be of tremendous benefit to the 15 per cent of the workforce who also care for someone needing special attention at home. The 1995 *Carers in Employment* report concluded that the likelihood of becoming a carer rises with age, so that carers are generally among an organisation's most experienced and valued members of staff[5]. According to the report, flexible working hours and part-time work are the options most frequently requested by carers. A further report by the Institute for Employment Studies (IES), previously known as the Institute of Manpower Studies (IMS), has revealed that approximately 5 per cent of employees take one day's sick leave each month to care for a dependent relative – which can represent a significant cost to the employer[6].

Part-time working can also be an effective way of retaining the skills of older, more experienced employees while building the skills of younger workers. Older staff may welcome the opportunity to work fewer hours as they prepare for retirement; the resultant salary savings can be used to hire younger employees, who can be trained to take over the older workers' jobs in due course.

Encouraging diversity and equality

Over the past 25 years the UK and other EU governments have become increasingly aware of the fact that 'traditional' working patterns not only penalise some sectors of the workforce but can also result in the skills they offer being underused. In response, legislation to redress the balance has been introduced to help various groups.

The Equal Pay and Sex Discrimination Acts of the 1970s have attempted to redress the balance in favour of women. The Equal Pay Act 1970 covers discrimination in pay and other contractual terms where there is a comparable man in the same employment. The Sex Discrimination Act 1975 covers discrimination outside the contract of employment – in training, transfers, promotion, and discretionary benefits. The Race Relations Act 1976 considers the needs of ethnic minorities – including, in some circumstances, religious needs. And the Disability Discrimination Act 1995 aims to facilitate the recruitment and retention of disabled workers.

As the emphasis on recruiting young staff increases, 'age discrimination' (which can adversely affect people as young as 35 in some sectors!) is increasingly becoming a matter of concern to the UK government. Although no legislation is planned, a code of practice – which employers will be expected to use as a guide in their dealings with older workers – has been issued.

Women and part-time working

Four in every five part-timers are women, and 79 per cent of this group say they choose to work part-time primarily because of family responsibilities (eg the care of children or elderly relatives). Opportunities to work part-time, to job-share or to work flexible hours are crucial to women's participation in the labour force. A refusal to facilitate such arrangements may be interpreted under the Sex Discrimination Act as 'indirect discrimination', ie the application of a requirement or condition that has an unequal impact on men and women. Because women are generally the primary carers of children and the elderly, a requirement to work full-time may be one that fewer women than men can meet. For this reason, it may be indirectly discriminatory to refuse part-time working to a woman returning from maternity leave.

Ethnic minorities

While rigid working hours generally discriminate against women, they may also discriminate indirectly on the grounds of race where an individual needs to be away from work for prayer times and religious holidays.

The Commission for Racial Equality (CRE) recommends that, where cultural and religious needs conflict with existing work requirements, employers should consider whether they can adapt their requirements to accommodate such needs.

Disabled employees

Unlike the earlier legislation discussed above, the Disability Discrimination Act applies only to employers with 15 or more staff. Within such establishments it covers anyone with a physical or mental impairment which has a substantial (i.e. not minor or trivial) and long-term adverse effect (basically lasting at least 12 months) upon his or her ability to carry out normal day-to-day activities.

The Act requires employers to take 'reasonable steps' to accommodate disabled employees. Among the examples given in section 6 (3) of the Act are:

- altering a disabled person's working hours
- allowing the disabled person to be absent during working hours for rehabilitation, assessment or treatment.

Taking such steps can help to retain workers who become disabled. The winter 1997/98 *Labour Force Survey* showed there were just over two million economically active people with a long-term health problem or disability in Great Britain[7]. It also revealed that nearly five million people of working age judge themselves to be covered by the Disability Discrimination Act's definition of disability, including just under one million who are not currently working but would like to do so.

Older workers

With the growing awareness of the discrimination faced by older workers, the government signalled its intention to support them by issuing a discussion document and proposed code of practice. The document pointed out that, by the year 2000, 35 per cent of the labour force will be aged over 45, rising to almost 40 per cent by 2010, whereas 16–24-year-olds will then make up just 17 per cent of the labour force.

Among other things, the government (through the Department for Education and Employment) recommends that employers should[8]:

- consider alternatives to early retirement for those whose skills and abilities may be lost
- use flexible retirement schemes where this is possible
- use phased retirement where possible to allow employees to alter the balance of their working and personal lives and prepare for full retirement. This can also help the business to prepare for the loss of employees' skills.

Making part-time employment more widely available can be instrumental in achieving these objectives.

Further considerations

It is insufficient simply to state that working less than full-time is impossible in your business. As far back as 1984 an industrial tribunal (*Home Office* v *Holmes*) established that an employer must justify his reasons. And more recently it was held (in *Barrett* v *Newport BC* 1991) that a blanket policy against flexible working, where no account is taken of individual circumstances, can also be unlawful. Nor can continuity of client relationships be relied upon as a justification for full-time working. In *Todd* v *Rushcliffe* (also 1991) the tribunal found this argument unjustified. Even full-timers are regularly absent on holiday or through sickness. Recent and ongoing developments in such technologies as faxes and mobile phones, which enable employees to keep in touch when not at work, would probably make the argument even weaker today.

Allowing staff to work less than full-time is only half the

story, however. In addition an employer should consider such aspects as training, appraisal, promotion and any other benefits routinely offered to full-time workers. Training opportunities, for example, are often offered to those employees considered to be a good investment – frequently those who work long hours. Training courses themselves often involve long hours at a residential location – both potential barriers to part-timers. Promotion is usually based on evidence of ambition, and it is frequently assumed that part-time workers are less ambitious. Yet such procedures can be discriminatory. Clear and well-documented promotion criteria and procedures are advisable. Where an appraisal system exists, the Equal Opportunities Commission (EOC) recommends that assessment criteria are examined to ensure they are not unlawfully discriminatory, and that the scheme is monitored to assess how it is working in practice.

The Part-Time Workers Directive

The Equal Pay Act and Sex Discrimination Acts currently allow differential treatment of part-time and full-time staff where this can be justified on business grounds. The new Part-Time Workers Directive is likely to alter this.

A framework agreement setting out the general principles and minimum requirements relating to part-time work was adopted by the UK's European partners at the end of 1997 and extended to the UK in April 1998. Legislation passing through the Westminster Parliament in 1999 seeks to enable the Minister of State to issue regulations and a code of practice which must be incorporated into UK law by April 2000.

The purpose of the legislation is:

- to provide for the removal of discrimination against part-time workers and to improve the quality of part-time work
- to facilitate the voluntary development of part-time work and to contribute to the flexible organisation of working time in a manner that takes into account the needs of employers and workers.

The legislation applies to part-time workers who have a legally defined employment contract or employment relationship. The government may choose to exclude casual workers from the legislation, but it will have to review the exclusion periodically to ensure that the objective reasons for doing so remain valid.

The term 'part-time worker' in this context applies to an employee whose normal hours of work, calculated on a weekly basis or as an average over a period of employment of up to one year, are fewer than the normal hours of work of a comparable full-time worker. (A 'comparable full-time worker' is defined as a full-time employee in the same establishment having the same type of employment contract or relationship who is engaged in the same or similar work or occupation with due regard for other considerations, which may include seniority, qualifications and skills.) Where there is no comparable full-time worker, comparison is to be made in accordance with national law or practice.

In line with the purpose of the legislation:

- EU member states should identify and review obstacles of a legal or administrative nature that may

limit the opportunities for part-time work and, where appropriate, eliminate them
- social partners (ie trade unions and employers) should identify and review obstacles that may limit opportunities for part-time work and, where appropriate, eliminate them.

A worker's refusal to transfer from full-time to part-time or vice versa should not in itself constitute a valid reason for termination of employment. As far as possible, employers should give consideration to:

- requests by workers to transfer from full-time to part-time work that becomes available in the establishment
- requests by workers to transfer from part-time to full-time work or to increase their working time, should the opportunity arise
- the provision of timely information on the availability of part-time and full-time positions in the establishment in order to facilitate transfers from full-time to part-time or vice versa
- measures to facilitate access to part-time work at all levels of the enterprise, including skilled and managerial positions and, where appropriate, measures to facilitate access by part-time workers to vocational training to enhance career opportunities and occupational mobility
- the provision of appropriate information about part-time working in the enterprise to existing bodies representing workers.

Summary

You positively need a policy on part-time working because:

- employing part-time workers can enable a business to use the labour supply more effectively, thereby reducing costs
- offering part-time work increases the pool of candidates from which you can recruit
- allowing highly skilled or long-serving staff to work reduced hours will enable you to retain the expertise of people who might otherwise be forced to leave your employment owing to changes in their circumstances
- part-time working can provide employees with a means of preparing for full retirement while younger workers are trained to replace older staff
- more women than men find it difficult to work full-time – and refusing to allow part-time working without a sound business reason could be seen as discriminatory under the Sex Discrimination Act
- other aspects of your employment policies – such as access to training and promotion – could also be seen as discriminatory if they apply without sound business reasons only to full-time staff
- the new Part-Time Workers Directive, which will be incorporated into UK law by April 2000, is likely to place greater emphasis on the equal treatment of part-time and full-time workers.

References

1 IMC/Manpower plc. *Corporate Employment Strategies and Trends, 1997/98.*

2 *Labour Force Survey.* London, The Stationery Office, summer 1998.

3 New Ways to Work. *Time for Change: A guide to flexible work patterns for SMEs.* London, 1999.

4 Select Committee on Education and Employment. *Part-Time Working, Second Report.* London, 1999.

5 Princess Royal Trust for Carers. *Carers in Employment.* London, 1995.

6 Institute of Manpower Studies. *Who Cares? The business benefits of carer-friendly policies.* Brighton, 1997.

7 *Labour Force Survey.* London, The Stationery Office, winter 1998.

8 Department for Education and Employment. *Advantage: Consultation on a code of practice for age diversity in employment.* London, DfEE, 1998.

How do I create a policy on part-time workers?

> ☑ Identifying the need and the business benefits
> ☑ Drafting a new policy and reviewing existing procedures
>   Recruitment – Compensation – Transfer between part-time and full-time work – Promotion – Appraisal – Training and development – Grievance/appeals – Retirement – Redundancy
> ☑ Publicising the policy and ensuring its purpose is understood
> ☑ Supporting implementation and monitoring the policy's impact
> ☑ Check-list

It takes time getting from the realisation that you need a policy on part-time workers to the point where that policy has been developed and accepted within the enterprise and is working well. Broadly, there are four stages you have to work through:

1 identifying the need for the policy and (very importantly) the business benefits that the policy will bring
2 drafting the policy and reviewing its effect on existing procedures (which may need to be amended)

3 publicising the policy and ensuring that all employees understand its purpose

4 supporting implementation of the policy and monitoring its impact on your business.

Identifying the need and the business benefits

If you find yourself receiving requests from staff who wish to work part-time, you will already be aware of the need for a policy on the matter. If you do not receive any such requests, then we suggest that the best place to start is by asking your staff. For a small employer this may simply mean talking with them face to face. In larger organisations more formal mechanisms exist, such as suggestion schemes or employee surveys, which can be used to assess demand.

When talking to staff, be sensitive to the culture of your organisation. In some cultures part-time working is seen as synonymous with low commitment or little ambition. Staff may be wary of expressing an interest in working part-time if they feel they might be penalised for saying so. In addition to talking directly with them it is wise to look at the composition of your workforce and consider how many of them may have outside commitments that would be easier to manage if they could work fewer hours. It is commonly accepted that mothers (particularly of pre-school children) welcome the opportunity to work part-time, but there may also be benefits for other groups of workers.

Older workers, for example, might welcome the chance to 'wind down' to retirement. And, if you have several employees working less than full-time, you can use the salary savings to recruit younger full-time successors who can be trained alongside them. Employees without children may have some other caring responsibility – perhaps for an elderly relative. The burden of coping with this as well as full-time work is also likely to be greater for single employees. Other employees may welcome the chance to work fewer hours while they pursue a course of study or take a more active role in their local community.

In addition to reviewing the needs of current staff you should consider whether offering part-time work will enable you to attract and recruit from a wider pool. This is particularly important if you are operating in an area of skills shortages or in a competitive market with inflationary salaries.

Finally, but most importantly, you must establish the business benefits to your organisation of encouraging part-time working. This will be the motivator that is most likely to encourage your senior managers to support the policy during the early days. For example, a core value at Littlewoods is to maintain 'equality of opportunity and dignity at work'. In line with this commitment, employees can work reduced hours in a number of patterns, such as term-time working and job-sharing. Business plans for each unit have a corresponding equality action plan, the business rationale being demonstrated through turnover figures and illustrations of the cost benefits of a pro-active staff-retention policy. Line managers are supported in making changes, and pilot schemes are conducted to demonstrate how re-organised work schedules can operate in practice.

Drafting a new policy and reviewing your existing procedures

The decision about how long or short your policy should be, whether it should be supported by procedures and how it should be worded depends to some extent on how existing policies have been structured. Some (typically large) organisations favour detailed, complex policies supported by procedural documents preparing for every eventuality. At the opposite extreme, your policy could be a simple one-line statement that the organisation supports part-time working. Either way, it is a good idea to have the policy written down and displayed where employees can see it. That way misunderstandings and misinterpretations may be avoided.

If starting from scratch with no other policies to use as guidelines, you may find the following suggestions useful:

- Establish what the goal of the finished policy (and procedures, if you choose to have them) will be. What is the desired result? What will happen if the policy is successful?
- Decide what part-time arrangements the policy will support. This depends on the demands of your business. Unless there are very good reasons to the contrary, you should also consider stating that the policy covers staff at all grades and in all jobs. This will help to overcome objections that 'part-time working is not possible at this level, or in this job'. In reality, very few jobs cannot operate on some sort of part-time arrangement.

- Consider the audience. Are they used to reading, understanding and acting upon policy documents? Do they like detailed procedures or do they prefer flexibility?
- Talk to people who may be able to help to develop your thinking. If you have colleagues in other organisations that already have a policy on part-timers, find out about their experience and consider whether it can be applied to your situation. If your organisation has a union presence, talk to the representatives. If any informal arrangements already exist in the organisation, talk to the managers and staff involved.
- Consult the managers who will implement the policy about what they feel *they* need to know. Produce a draft policy and consult them again. In doing so you will be involving them at the planning stage: they will therefore be able to help to identify any problems that might limit the policy's effectiveness, and they will be more likely to feel that they 'own' the policy. When the final policy is produced, they will be familiar with its content and less likely to resist implementation. For example, the Cheshire Health Agency involves a high proportion of its 128 staff in the review of policies and in contributing ideas early in the development stage of new initiatives.

Once you have finalised your policy you will need to consider its effect on existing policies and practices in your business. Let's now look at a few of these.

Recruitment

The recruitment policy may need to be amended to include a statement about which jobs will be offered on a part-time or job-share basis. Recruitment practices may also need to be reviewed to enable you to reach new groups of potential employees wishing to work part-time: for example, additional advertising in local newspapers and job centres will reach those people who assume that jobs advertised in national newspapers are always full-time. The Women Returners' Network can also advise on recruitment (their details are included in the *Resources* section of this book).

Compensation

The pay and benefits policy may need to be amended to make it clear that all benefits will be pro rata for part-timers. Where you provide such benefits as private health or dental care you may need to talk with insurers about the cost implications. You may feel that this is an appropriate moment to introduce a flexible benefits package so that employees can tailor benefits to their own needs.

If you pay overtime, it is important to clarify when an employee will become eligible to receive it. In many organisations part-timers are required to work extra hours up to those of full-timers on basic rates in order to become eligible.

Transfer between part-time and full-time work

Whereas some employees may want to work reduced hours permanently, working part-time may for others be a short-term option. You may need a policy on how and when staff can transfer between part-time and full-time work, and vice versa. For example, splitting a job into two takes time, and changing employee hours can create extra administrative work. You may, therefore, wish to restrict the number of changes that a particular employee is able to make in the course of a year, or ask for a period of notice when requests are being made.

Promotion

The basis on which employees are promoted, particularly if an ability to work full-time or having so worked for a certain number of years is currently a requirement, may need to be reconsidered. This could be an appropriate time to move towards a competency-based approach to promotion and appraisal.

Appraisal

It is a mistake to assume that staff working part-time are not interested in receiving feedback about performance and progress. They should be included in the appraisal process. However, appraisal documentation may need revision to ensure the system is easy to understand, operate and monitor. Managers should be trained to understand the importance of consistent and defensible judgements of subordinates. They should be encouraged to judge performance on the quality of outputs rather than time spent in the workplace. You could also consider moving towards the appraisal of competencies that can be gained in various ways, rather than simply looking at on-the-job experience (which may in any case be less relevant if yours is a fast-changing business environment).

Training and development

It pays to involve part-timers in training and teambuilding exercises – don't leave them out simply on the assumption that they are less committed to their work. However, you may need to reconsider how to make training available to them. If it is currently delivered mostly as residential courses, perhaps you could consider alternatives. Some employers, for example, pay childcare or eldercare expenses during training courses or for other work commitments outside normal hours. If you have sufficient numbers of part-timers, perhaps the timing of the course could be altered to accommodate their needs; or perhaps an alternative, such as distance learning, could be offered.

If you provide full-time staff with training during their working hours, you should do the same with part-timers, or pay them for the additional hours they attend any training over and above the normal hours worked.

Grievance/appeals

You should consider incorporating something into grievance and appeals procedures that gives part-time staff the right to protest if they feel unfairly treated because of their part-time status and to appeal if their request to work part-time is denied. Alternatively, this can be included in the main part-time working policy.

Retirement

Phased retirement can be an attractive option for older employees and can be of benefit to the business. If you choose to offer part-time working in these circumstances, check the pensions implications. The Employers' Forum on Age can offer further advice.

Redundancy

Finally, redundancy procedures – particularly the guidelines for selection for redundancy – should be reviewed to ensure that part-time staff are treated equally alongside full-timers. The fact that someone is working part-time or that, as a result of so doing, he has less actual service should not in itself be a reason for selecting him first for redundancy.

Publicising the policy and ensuring its purpose is understood

If you have been consulting with managers and staff as you develop the policy, its introduction should come as no surprise to them. However, don't assume that everyone is aware of its existence. Use whatever communications strategies are in place in your business to provide information about the new policy to all employees.

Communicate the business reasons for its introduction, what changes you expect as a result and where staff may go for further information. If resistance is likely then consider a 'bedding-in' period between introducing the policy and its becoming fully effective (ie you introduce the policy on 1 January and say it will become fully effective on 1 March). Such change should be a gradual process: many people need time to adjust to new ways of working.

To ensure the policy's success it is essential to train managers. They may well have concerns about the negative impact that part-time working could have on their workload. They may feel that staff will be harder to control or that the quality of work in the department will suffer. Many of these fears are likely to be groundless. But it is important to recognise them as genuine concerns and to provide support in managing the transition.

Ensure that managers fully understand the perceived business benefits of introducing the new policy. If they are convinced of them they will be more likely to support the policy. They may benefit from time-management or self-management training to help them in managing a more flexible group of employees. You could also incorporate into appraisals questions about how successfully they manage part-time staff. This will both emphasise the importance of the issue and provide a means of assessing how well managers are coping. For example, management training programmes at BT now include modules on work–life issues, while 'valuing diversity' workshops seek to underline the message that everyone is different and has a different contribution to make. The workshops also seek to remind managers that people have home commitments and that some may have caring responsibilities.

Supporting implementation and monitoring the policy's impact

The first people to apply for part-time working in your organisation (especially if they are in such areas as senior management) are likely to be viewed as pioneers by the rest of the workforce. They will be feeling their way – as will their own managers – so extra support is likely to be needed at this time. How you deal with these early cases will affect take-up in other parts of your organisation. Flexibility and regular reviews and feedback will help in these early stages when they (and you) are entering uncharted territory. The whole organisation will be learning together, so it is important for all staff involved to know that they have the confidence and backing of senior management during this transition phase.

In drafting the policy you should have identified desirable outcomes. These may be in the form of numerical targets: for example, '10 per cent of staff will be working part-time or 3 per cent of jobs will be shares'. We recommend that progress against these targets be reviewed six months after the policy has been introduced, and thereafter at regular intervals.

Don't be surprised if take-up is slow to begin with. It takes time for people to make the adjustment. It may be easier to recruit part-timers than to encourage current employees to work part-time. (If you do this, it is important to support the new recruits while the organisation adjusts to their presence.) It can also be helpful to monitor such aspects as turnover and retention. Are you losing fewer staff because you now offer part-time work? Are you able to schedule work more effectively – perhaps avoiding overtime costs?

If interest remains low after the first year, take steps to find out why and to make any necessary adjustments. As we said at the start of this chapter, arriving at an effective policy for part-timers can be a slow process, but if you are clear about the business benefits it will gather momentum over time.

Check-list

- Is there a demand for part-time working among your existing and potential employees?

39

- Are you clear about the business benefits of offering part-time work?
- What do you hope to achieve by developing and introducing a policy on part-time working?
- Have you identified what part-time arrangements will be most appropriate to your circumstances?
- Are there people within your organisation or outside it who already have experience of part-time working and who can help you to develop your thinking?
- Have you consulted the managers who will be responsible for implementing the new policy and identified their concerns and reservations?
- Have you considered the impact the new policy will have on existing employment policies?
- Do you have a strategy to publicise the new policy widely among employees?
- Have you planned training for managers to help them to understand the benefits of the new policy and how they can best implement it?
- Do you have a strategy for supporting 'pioneers'?
- Have you set a realistic timetable for evaluating how well the policy is operating in practice and for making necessary adjustments?

How do I recruit and retain part-time workers?

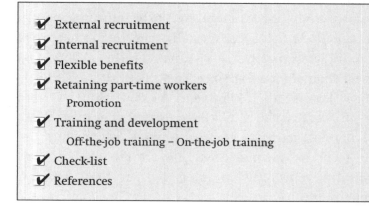

☑ External recruitment
☑ Internal recruitment
☑ Flexible benefits
☑ Retaining part-time workers
   Promotion
☑ Training and development
   Off-the-job training – On-the-job training
☑ Check-list
☑ References

You may well find that one business benefit of having part-time workers is that you broaden your recruitment pool, attracting a larger number of applicants in the process. In this chapter we look particularly at external and internal recruitment, flexible benefits, and training and development.

External recruitment

Recent research by Roffey Park Management Institute has revealed that even organisations with sophisticated recruitment and selection procedures for full-time staff do not always follow the same processes or adopt the same rigour when recruiting flexible employees[1]. Insufficient attention is given to understanding the needs and expectations of flexible workers at the selection stage. Roffey Park recommend that managers be honest about what a job entails and what expectations they have. Honesty from applicants is also essential for successful recruitment, so it is important that interviewers work to encourage this.

The most significant difference between those looking for full-time work and those looking for part-time is that the latter group is much more likely to be returning to work after a period of absence. Typically they are mothers with childcare responsibilities or carers of the elderly and infirm. Their enforced absence from the workplace is likely to have lowered their confidence in their abilities. More likely to feel that their skills are outdated, they may choose to avoid contacting large organisations, which they perceive to be too intimidating. They are less likely to 'sell themselves' effectively at interview. For these reasons, employer involvement in 'back to work' schemes can be very successful. During the period of a scheme, returners have an opportunity to learn more about potential employers who, in turn, are able to evaluate scheme participants. The Industrial Society has been involved in helping employers to establish such schemes and can offer advice and guidance. Alternatively, if you know of a scheme already running in your area – perhaps in a local college of further education – you can contact them for details of how you could be involved.

Recruitment fairs can also be an effective way of targeting particular geographic or social groups seeking work. In addition, contact with the local community can be a powerful PR exercise for your business. Large employers (such as the major food retailers) will typically use a recruitment fair to staff an enterprise in a new location. For smaller employers it can be more effective to band together with other small employers in the area that have similar vacancies. The local Chamber of Commerce can usually offer help and advice on setting up a recruitment fair.

Should you decide to advertise your vacancies, you will need to tailor the media to suit your audience. For more senior positions, where people already in work may be looking for promotion on a part-time basis, national newspapers and trade press are appropriate. Your advertisement should state clearly that the job is being offered on a part-time basis. If you are offering a job-share (see Chapter 6) you should indicate whether applicants need to have a job-share partner or whether you will recruit one for them. (It is, of course, always possible that you will be looking for one half of a job-share only after having responded to an internal request by a current member of staff.)

Less skilled workers looking for part-time work may need to be reached in other ways. You can widen your search by:

- notifying the local job centre – but be aware that not all job-seekers use this service (women in particular tend to use alternative methods of finding work)
- advertising in local newspapers
- sending a targeted mailing to a local or community group (eg a local playgroup or residents association)
- contacting local training organisations with return-to-work courses.

The evidence suggests that many part-time workers are well

qualified, yet it is often the case that, in order to secure part-time work, they need to accept jobs below their skill levels. Nevertheless, before advertising you should consider whether the skills and experience you are asking for are absolutely necessary for the jobs on offer. Check also that any application form you may be using is relevant, not too long and does not ask seemingly irrelevant questions.

When interviewing prospective employees, don't overlook the skills and experience they may have gained through unpaid or voluntary work. Many of these skills have been shown to overlap with those required in paid work, particularly in service occupations. The interview is also the place to clarify all the arrangements for the job, thus avoiding any future misunderstandings. For example, if the job is part-time, what hours will the applicant be expected to work? Will he or she be required to do regular overtime? Will the overtime be paid at standard or premium rates?

Internal recruitment

Some existing employees may be keen to work fewer than full-time hours. The most likely groups to show an interest are new mothers returning to work and those with other caring responsibilities. However, there are a number of other reasons why staff may want to work part-time:

- because of a disability that limits how many hours they feel able to work
- because they wish to pursue a course of further education or become involved in voluntary or community activities

- because they are nearing retirement and wish to develop a wider portfolio of interests.

One respondent to a major survey into part-time working listed the benefits that she had experienced[2]:

> I have worked a part-time working pattern between 12 and 27 hours [a week] for the past 13 years. It has enabled me:
> a) to be available to my children when they were at school
> b) to care for my mother, who developed Alzheimer's Disease
> and now
> c) to begin a degree course.

For more senior employees, job-sharing is becoming a more accepted way of introducing part-time hours into jobs that have traditionally been available only on a full-time basis. This is a way of working where two people voluntarily share the responsibilities of one full-time job. The advantage to the organisation is that the job continues to exist in its full-time format, and a full-time employee can be moved into it at some later stage. In some positions, job-splitting (where two people divide the tasks of one job between them with minimum co-ordination) may be more appropriate or easier for the organisation to manage. Further information about creating part-time jobs, job-sharing and job-splitting can be found in Chapter 6.

Company communications media such as noticeboards, in-house magazines and intranets can be used to advertise part-time vacancies and to look for job-share partners where appropriate. Publicising part-time options widely serves to create a powerful internal message about the organisation's commitment to part-time working.

Flexible benefits

An important aspect of most recruitment and retention strategies is the benefits package offered alongside pay. Traditional packages were based on the model of a full-time male employee with a wife and family at home. In the last few years, however, flexible benefits plans that allow employees to choose the benefits they find most useful have become more popular. According to a recent survey there are now around 100 flexible benefits plans operating in the UK[3]. Increasingly more emphasis is being placed on benefits such as dental insurance, critical illness insurance, health screening and childcare, with less focus on cars. A further benefit sometimes included in flexible packages is the ability to trade pay for extra holiday, which can be very attractive to those trying to balance work and caring responsibilities.

Benefits consultants maintain that a major advantage for employers is the better targeting of benefits to meet employee needs. Consequently, benefits are more highly valued, making the total compensation package more competitive. In addition, consultants suggest that, through an analysis of the choices made, offering a flexible package can provide more information about employee needs.

Retaining part-time workers

Retaining any group of employees is a complex process of understanding their needs at work and ensuring that these are met. This can include the need to develop and to progress, to be well managed and to be treated fairly by the organisation. We shall consider some of these issues – particularly those relating to training, development and promotion – in this chapter and the rest in Chapter 5.

There are two main reasons why the needs of part-time staff are likely to differ from those of full-timers:

- because of the outside work commitments that push them into part-time work
- because of organisational difficulties that can arise as a result of working less than full-time.

It is important to remember an obvious truth – that organisations and individuals change over time. Having a forum to discuss changing needs at a personal, team and organisational level is important. For example, Littlewoods is creating a culture where employees feel comfortable talking about work–life issues that may affect performance. To facilitate this, the company runs focus groups, employee climate surveys, open forums and even meals with the CEO.

There is a widespread perception that working more flexibly calls for greater organisational abilities and managerial time, both for arranging staff meetings and for appraising staff. Reassuringly, an IES study carried out in 1992 found that in many organisations this was seen merely as a 'teething problem'. Organisations with a history of flexible work arrangements had worked out effective lines of communication and hand-over procedures[4].

Promotion

It is as wrong to assume that part-timers are not interested in promotion as it is to assume that all full-time staff are.

Many flexible workers would welcome promotion as a natural dimension of the strong commitment they feel towards their work. (For example, in their survey of flexible working at senior levels, New Ways to Work found that 40 out of 106 respondents had been with the same employer for between 10 and 28 years – representing a major commitment from employees and considerable investment on the part of employers.)

Where part-time employees seek promotion it may be possible to offer a job-share arrangement. If the two halves of the share perform well, it is also possible to promote them into a new post together.

Training and development

Investing in training part-timers has traditionally been seen as more costly than training their full-time colleagues, because there is a lower return in terms of hours worked. Nevertheless, as far back as 1989 the (then) Department of Employment was recommending (through the Training Agency) that employers stop concentrating their training activities solely on core full-time employees in order to address workforce skill needs. And a 1994 survey revealed that training part-timers led to better service, increased sales turnover and managers who felt more confident and comfortable about staff competence. In addition it improved motivation, commitment, enthusiasm and staff-retention, with the conclusion that 'training part-timers is regarded as good value for money'[5].

Larger companies, particularly those in sectors with high customer-contact, are now recognising the benefit of training part-timers. For example, Marks and Spencer – with a workforce that is two-thirds part-time – say that they treat their part-time and full-time staff the same way. Indeed, returners and carers – who form the majority of part-timers – tend to be a very stable section of the workforce. They are usually grateful for the opportunity to work less than full-time and are unlikely to move so long as their needs for flexibility are being met. For example, SEI Macro is a small company in the semiconductor distribution industry, where high staff turnover is the norm. Following the introduction of a range of reduced and flexible working options, the company has received feedback from staff that suggests they are more committed to their jobs than before and less likely to leave, because the same options are not available elsewhere.

Evidence suggests that female part-timers are more likely to be overqualified for their current jobs than either male or female full-timers. This is owing both to their own tendency to undervalue their skills following a period away from the labour market and to the fact that they are generally obliged to take jobs at lower levels than the ones they held previously as a trade-off for more flexibility. At the same time, they often do not expect to be offered training and may worry that asking for any may reflect badly on them. In addition, low-paid female workers often lack the incentive to train because of a lack of confidence in their ability, fear of change, anxiety about supervising others and fear of increased responsibility.

Even in organisations with a strong commitment to training, central messages can sometimes fail to reach branch levels, where line managers have relative autonomy about the training provided for staff. Such managers sometimes act on widely held but erroneous assumptions which can have a detrimental effect on the amount of training offered to particular groups of employees. Such erroneous assumptions include the following:

- It is not worth training older workers.
- There is no need to provide more training for people in low-level jobs.
- People who work part-time are less committed to their work.
- People working part-time are not interested in training and development.
- Part-time workers tend to have low skill-levels.
- Part-time workers have free time that they can devote to training.

It is important that employers address and correct these mistaken beliefs so that the potential of the entire work-force can be fully developed regardless of age or status. As one respondent to a major survey into changing work patterns (a woman in her late 30s) put it[6]:

> I have recently been told that, although I have the qualifications, both academic and practical, I will need to increase my working commitment should I wish to advance my career. With an 18-month-old, and a four-year-old about to start school, I feel they are my priority to the detriment of personal achievements, despite the skills I can offer.

Finally, excluding part-timers from access to training may be deemed discriminatory if those part-time workers are predominantly female. This is particularly important where attendance at training courses may be a prerequisite for promotion.

Off-the-job-training

The most common form of training reported in *Labour Force Surveys* is the off-the-job kind. When planning this type of training for part-time staff, bear these points in mind:

- Part-timers often lack the time to pursue courses, usually because of the very commitments that lead them into part-time work. Some are able to attend courses only in the evenings, when partners can help with childcare but when less training is available. Employers' help with child- or eldercare costs can often make attendance at daytime training courses easier.

- Part-timers working irregular or unsociable (eg night) shifts may be overlooked or forgotten when training is being planned or scheduled.

- It is important to give part-timers the same induction training and the same welcome as full-timers so that they understand they are valuable members of staff.

- Many smaller employers are unaware of what might be available in their local community to support employees wishing to undertake training. The local Training and Enterprise Council (TEC) or Chamber of Commerce can provide information about this.

- Learning is becoming increasingly 'modular' through the development of training 'units' which can be linked together as appropriate. This not only makes it easier for employers and their staff to customise training but also provides a greater opportunity to include part-timers in continuing training. Individual training 'modules' can be scheduled to fit in with the employees' work schedules.

- Some large employers (particularly in the banking, retail and manufacturing sectors) have introduced on-site learning centres where 'open' and 'distance' learning packages can be used by staff at times convenient to them. The use both of packages and learning centres is becoming increasingly popular.
- National Vocational Qualifications (NVQs) are an effective way of encouraging the formalisation of on-the-job training. Boots, for example, has a company-wide policy of encouraging all shop-floor staff to study and train for a qualification in retailing up to NVQ Level 2. They see this as 'a recipe for greater retention, commitment and personal development'[7].
- Combining team meetings with training events can be a very effective use of limited time. Attendance at training sessions is boosted, and it can lead people to see how training is being integrated into the job role. Learning alongside other team members can also have beneficial outcomes.

On-the-job-training

According to Michael Eraut, Professor of Education at Sussex University, 'continuing formal education and training provide only a small part of what is learned at work'[8]. The workplace also offers many opportunities for learning on the job. Here are some examples:

- Membership of a special task group performing a review, an audit or the preparation of a policy. It is likely that the part-timer's experience, being dissimilar to that of full-time colleagues, may also serve to add value to the process and increase its benefit to the organisation.

- Job rotation, cross-training or even a secondment. Encouraging such multiskilling in part-timers can result in more efficient cover arrangements, add interest to the job and encourage loyalty. For example, Market Monitor, a telesales company with just 26 employees, has developed a multiskilled approach to the needs of their work. This has enabled staff to cover for each other when necessary, and has resulted in increased confidence, especially among new employees and women returners.
- Attendance at a relevant conference or meeting (where this can be appropriately scheduled), with a requirement to report back to fellow workers or management.
- Being mentored or coached, or acting as mentor or coach to a more junior member of staff.

Professor Eraut points out that much of the informal learning that happens in organisations involves keeping abreast of developments or consulting colleagues in other areas for expert advice or information. It is important, therefore, that part-timers are given the opportunity to network in this manner during working hours.

Adopting a more flexible approach to training and development starts with more emphasis on planning a personal development strategy. This can be a valuable part of the appraisal discussion, to be considered further in the next chapter.

Check-list

- Have recruitment and selection procedures – including the application form, selection criteria and interview techniques – been reviewed to ensure their appropriateness for recruiting part-timers?
- Have alternative methods of recruitment, such as job fairs, contact with returners' courses and mailings to local groups, been considered?
- Is there a procedure for ensuring that all relevant arrangements are discussed at interview to avoid future misunderstandings?
- For more skilled or senior staff, could job-sharing be a viable alternative to full-time work?
- Would offering a flexible benefits package help to recruit and to retain staff?
- Do any existing employees wish to work part-time? If so, how can they reduce their hours?
- Does your business have a forum for employees to discuss their changing needs?
- Does the training and development policy apply equally to full-time and part-time staff?
- Do managers who control training budgets understand and apply the organisation's policy on training?
- Are part-timers given the same induction training and made to feel as welcome and as valued as full-timers?
- Can formal training be restructured to accommodate the needs of part-timers?
- Do on-the-job training opportunities exist for part-timers to develop their skills?

● Are part-timers eligible for promotion? If promoted, can they continue to work part-time?

References

1 EVANS C. 'Managing the flexible workforce successfully'. *Training Officer*. Vol. 34, No. 8, October 1998. pp 241–4.
2 TMP WORLDWIDE. *The Flexible Workforce – Fact or Fiction? A major survey into the realities of new working patterns*. London, TMP, 1998.
3 WATSON WYATT. *Strategic Rewards Survey*. London, 1998.
4 SIMKIN C. *and* HILLAGE J. *Family Friendly Working: New hope or old hype?* Report 224. Brighton, IES, 1992.
5 HALL L. 'On course for equality'. *Personnel Today*. 17 May 1994. pp 33–4.
6 See reference no.2 above.
7 McGIVNEY V. *Wasted Potential: Training and career progression for part-time and temporary workers*. Leicester, National Institute of Adult Continuing Education, 1994.
8 ERAUT M. 'Learning in the workplace'. *Training Officer*. Vol. 34, No. 6. July–August 1998. pp 172–4.

How do I manage part-time workers?

The changing role of managers

Economic turbulence over the last two decades has thrown into confusion the expectations that organisations have of their managers. The new management role frequently encompasses those of leader, coach, facilitator, counsellor and, at times, co-worker. Reductions in organisational hierarchies have also resulted in fewer managers doing more work and supervising more people. For the small-business owner–manager, life is even tougher. In addition to embracing a wide-ranging people-management role, he or she has to juggle numerous other commercial roles equally essential to the growth of a business. Businesses of all sizes are increasingly expected to operate longer opening hours in response to customer needs. The efficient use of part-time staff is a good way of ensuring that this is done cost-effectively.

Although the purpose of this chapter is to look at the management of part-time workers, a broader reflection on the role of the manager is appropriate. What is required of that role differs from business to business and, in some organisations, it will be up to the individual to define his or her own role. However it is done, achieving a degree of role clarity is essential to being a successful manager. If *you* do not know what is expected of you, how can you define what you expect of your staff?

Investing time in making sure that your management style has kept up with changing working practices pays dividends in the long run. Well-managed employees are likely to be more productive and to work more effectively as a team.

How do part-timers want to be managed?

Research by Roffey Park Management Institute suggests that part-timers would like their managers to[1]:

- be flexible in understanding the constraints they are under (in terms of home commitments) and take these into account when scheduling work
- be flexible in allowing individuals to change their

hours in the event of an emergency at home

- be approachable and prepared to 'roll their sleeves up' when necessary, and make time to listen to staff problems, to offer advice and to provide support
- allow them scope and encouragement to develop their skills by varying the tasks they are required to do, or by giving them specific areas of responsibility
- trust them to complete tasks in a way that works best for them, and provide them with regular feedback on performance
- communicate with them regularly to ensure that they are up to date with developments in the workplace
- adopt a more consistent approach to training and development (this was discussed in the previous chapter).

In addition, part-time staff say that they want to feel challenged in their work, to share ideas on how to improve the business operation and to feel that their contribution is recognised.

The Institute's study concentrated on part-timers, but it is very likely that a group of full-time employees would list the same things. The list is long, but responding to at least some of these needs could make you a better all-round manager and bring rewards in the long term.

Essential management skills

Part-time staff need to be managed in exactly the same way as full-timers. By investing in your part-time employees, you will reap the dividends in the longer term.

Four skills are essential to good management:

- communication
- time management
- assertiveness
- resourcefulness.

There is a perception that managing staff who are working non-standard hours may require extra management time. This is often true in the short term as the organisation adapts to new ways of working. On the positive side, once it decides to alter its working patterns a business has the opportunity to review and improve its existing systems.

Communication

Effective communication is the most essential skill when it comes to managing staff – particularly where they are working non-standard hours. Survey after survey reveals communication to be one of the most problematic areas for part-timers, despite the phenomenal growth in communications technology within many organisations. In addition to noticeboards and in-house newspapers, many businesses can now communicate with employees via e-mail or an intranet. 'Senior posts can be worked flexibly provided that all concerned are fully flexible and provided that lines of communication are effective[2].

A clear business need exists for part-timers to be as well informed as their full-time colleagues, particularly where this affects customer service. Feeling they are missing out on information can make part-timers feel alienated and have an adverse effect on performance. It may even encourage them to leave. Good communication is also essential for fostering a teamwork culture – an increasingly popular way of working in many businesses.

Here are some real-life examples of ways in which communication with part-timers can be improved:

- A large retailer has introduced communications folders held by the cash desk. These contain information on sales targets and how well they are being met, personnel news and other key items.
- Another employer has introduced an overlapping shift arrangement in the form of a formal, paid, half-hour hand-over period. During this hand-over part-timers can update each other on operational changes, and outstanding tasks can be passed directly to another employee. This maintains continuity and ensures that tasks are completed satisfactorily. The hand-over period also provides an opportunity for part-timers to get to know each other and build a more collaborative working approach.
- A third employer 'twins' part-timers with a full-time partner who is responsible for ensuring that the part-timer hears about anything that may happen when he is not at work.

Time management

Time-management books and courses are prolific, and companies have to select a particular approach in which to train their managers. Unfortunately, not all human beings are alike and so any given course may not meet everybody's needs consequently many give up on the notion of time management. If you have yet to find a system that suits you we recommend you persevere. An effective time-management system will provide better control over your priorities and more balance in your working life.

Assertiveness

Being assertive means stating your wants, needs, ideas and opinions clearly and confidently. Doing so increases the chances that those needs will be met and that others will take notice of your opinions. Assertiveness also means paying attention to the needs and wishes of others and not dismissing or ignoring them. This in turn can encourage more open and honest communication with colleagues. There is, however, a difference between assertive and aggressive behaviour. Aggressive people are clear and forceful about their own needs but take no account of the needs and wants of others. Not only is this a recipe for making you a very unpopular manager, you could also find yourself accused of bullying or harassment.

Assertive communication with your own manager, particularly when discussing any difficulties you may be experiencing in your management role, is important. Unless your organisation receives feedback about the issues involved in managing part-time staff nothing can be done to improve the situation.

Resourcefulness

The pace of change in the workplace continues to intensify. Large organisations are subject to mergers and reorganisations, small ones grow rapidly or may be taken over. In these circumstances even experienced managers can sometimes find they need additional support. The resourceful manager will be able to identify when he needs additional help or information and how best to obtain this. For example, company policies and employment legislation can change very rapidly. You should feel comfortable that you know where to go for up-to-date information on these matters.

Strategies for including part-time workers

- Be honest at interview and on the first day about what the job entails and the level of flexibility expected. Some part-timers can be more flexible than others, depending on personal circumstances.
- Make sure that the new part-timer receives some form of induction to your department – and to the wider organisation, if appropriate.
- Remember to brief part-timers about relevant aspects of health and safety legislation. It is easy to overlook them when fulfilling your legal obligations to staff.
- Have a strategy for ensuring that part-timers know about events occurring and decisions made in their absence.
- Make sure that the rest of your department or team knows which members are working part-time, when they will be available and what impact the arrangement is likely to have on other staff.
- Wherever possible, ensure that team meetings or briefings are held at times when part-timers are working.
- Never assume that an individual has no interest in training and development simply because he is working part-time (see also Chapter 4).
- Consider whether you can restructure your department's work on a more flexible basis to incorporate part-timers fully into what is going on.

63

- Encourage occasions when the whole team can socialise together (for example, have a departmental lunch or arrange to have a drink after work).

Monitoring performance and appraising staff

Ensuring the day-to-day quality of subordinates' work is an important part of the manager's job. To do this successfully it is important to set clearly defined job objectives against which an employee's performance can be measured. As with full-time employees, any shortfalls in the performance of part-timers should be addressed as soon as they occur. This may prove more complicated if the individual is working an irregular pattern. Make arrangements to meet him at the first convenient opportunity (doing so by letter to the home address if necessary) outlining the reasons for the meeting. Allow the employee time to explain what happened (particularly if you did not witness the event yourself) before making any decision about remedial action.

It is reasonable to expect that your part-time workers will:

- provide you with a clear idea of the times when they will be available for work
- give as much notice as possible should outside commitments require a change in working hours
- co-operate in scheduling work and share responsibility for planning rotas
- keep colleagues advised of their hours and activities
- participate in team activities.

Appraisal meetings, on the other hand, provide a good

opportunity for taking a longer-term view, for establishing future plans and for identifying any difficulties (both work-related and as a result of home commitments). Many part-time workers are keen to develop careers. For some, this might involve becoming multiskilled, whereas others may wish to enhance technical or managerial skills in readiness for future promotion. The appraisal meeting is the place to develop plans for the forthcoming year that will enable them to achieve these goals.

It also provides a structured opportunity to review performance over the last year. In appraising the performance of part-time staff, a manager should take into account:

- the quality of departmental and organisational communication and control systems
- the circumstances in which the job is being carried out, particularly where the work was previously carried out on a full-time basis under different circumstances
- that it is generally more effective to agree targets the employee can achieve in his own way than to be prescriptive about procedures.

Appraising job-sharers can have its own complications. Organisations that have offered job-sharing for some time generally recognise that part of the appraisal process should consider how effectively the two sharers work together. In addition, setting objectives for the coming year will require the involvement of both partners. One suggestion is to appraise each sharer individually, and then follow up with a joint meeting to agree targets.

65

If you are a part-time manager . . .

Many organisations are demonstrating that part-time managers can be very successful. In most circumstances the key to success lies in *effective communication* – between you and your own manager, a job-share partner (if you have one), and your staff. Mobile telephones and e-mail mean that communication is possible in all but the most difficult circumstances.

It is important that all this communication is a two-way process, and that everyone understands it is their responsibility to make sure it works. Think creatively about how you can overcome communications difficulties and encourage your staff to do the same.

There will be some arrangements that are very difficult to manage, even with creative communication – such as where there is very little overlap between your hours and those of your subordinates. In such circumstances you may need to re-think your working arrangements and those of your department.

Check-list

- Are you clear about what is expected of you as a manager? If not, how will you be able to define your expectations of subordinates?
- Are you confident that you have the relevant skills to manage the demands of a part-time workforce (in particular *communication*, time management, assertiveness and resourcefulness)? If not, how can you develop the appropriate skills?
- Is your immediate line manager able to assist with guidance and support?

- Are there others in the organisation who can help (for example, the personnel department or another departmental manager who is also managing part-time staff)?
- Are there any external organisations that you can contact? (Refer to the resources list at the end of this book.)
- Are you happy that the part-time arrangements being worked in your department or team are appropriate to your business? (See Chapter 1 for a discussion of the range of part-time options.)
- Are your staff genuinely working part-time or are they trying to do a full-time job in reduced hours?
- Have the objectives and outcomes of part-time jobs been clearly defined and communicated to employees?
- Have your part-time staff been adequately briefed on relevant aspects of health and safety legislation?
- Do you have a strategy for ensuring that part-time staff are made aware of things that happen when they are not at work?
- Do you have a strategy for making sure that part-time staff feel included as part of the team?
- Have you included part-time staff in your department's training and development plans?
- Are part-timers eligible for regular appraisal? Is the appraisal process appropriate to their situation?

References

1 ROFFEY PARK MANAGEMENT INSTITUTE. *The Challenge of Managing the Part-time Workforce.* Horsham, RPMI, 1996.
2 NEW WAYS TO WORK. *Change at the Top: Working flexibly at senior and managerial levels in organisations.* London, 1993.

What else do I need to know?

☑ Creating part-time jobs
  Part-time working at senior levels – Work redesign
☑ Job-sharing and job-splitting
  Job-share or job-split? – How to make a job-share work
☑ Using technology to ease administration
☑ References

In this chapter we shall be looking at what else you need to know in order to recruit, retain and develop a part-time workforce, specifically:

- issues to consider in creating part-time jobs
- job-sharing and job-splitting
- how administration can be reduced with new technology.

Creating part-time jobs

An employer may make a strategic decision to create part-time jobs as a result of the perceived business benefits, or part-time working can occur by default and piecemeal in response to employee requests. A well-developed, business-based strategy will enable the employer to select the arrangements that are most appropriate to his business. A number of factors are likely to influence the decision:

- the nature of the business, its peaks and troughs and the timescales of the operation. For example, a retailer may be looking for increased staff cover at times when customers are most likely to shop, whereas a manufacturer may need to cover production peaks and troughs during a 24-hour, 7-day cycle.
- the types of jobs and attendant skill levels that make up the organisation. Although it is the authors' belief that almost every job can be worked on a more flexible basis, some (typically supervisory or managerial) will be more appropriate for job-sharing, whereas others (such as retail assistants or call-centre operators) lend themselves to part-time hours.
- the size of the enterprise. For example, reassigning tasks and activities may be easier in a large organisation, which has more employees to share the load.
- the reasons for introducing part-time work and whether they are as a result of recruitment difficulties, a desire to increase staff retention or a response to employee pressures. For example, although an employer may wish to split one job into two half-time jobs that he feels can be easily managed, an employee may prefer to work a reduced week of three or four days.

When introducing part-time arrangements in response to

workforce needs, bear in mind that different sectors of the workforce have different needs. As a rule, employers tend to be more understanding about the work–family conflicts of women, and so policies on flexible working tend to be aimed at them. But a survey of working men carried out by New Ways to Work in 1995 identified a growing demand among men for more flexibility to balance work and home lives[1]. Men are more likely to favour job-sharing as a means of working reduced hours while avoiding the perceived 'negative' status of being a part-timer. (It is also for this reason that employers are increasingly using such terms as 'key-time worker' to reflect the valuable contribution made by these employees.)

Part-time working at senior levels

Evidence suggests that part-time working at senior levels is becoming more common and more acceptable. For example, a recent survey by the Institute of Management found that 49 per cent of respondents had part-time employees in managerial and professional grades[2]. A further survey of 71 organisations in the public and private sectors carried out by IRS in 1997 found that a significant proportion employed part-time staff in highly skilled jobs[3]. The conclusion is that the image of part-time staff as uncommitted and second class is becoming outdated.

The evidence also calls into question commonly voiced objections that flexible working is not appropriate at the most senior organisational levels. For example, the 'Balanced Lives' survey conducted by New Ways to Work found a number of respondents were working at senior levels, and 40 per cent were involved in managing others. The highest full-time equivalent salary was £100,000, while six men were in jobs with full-time salaries between £30,000 and £60,000[4]:

> More than anything else, there is a need to re-examine the assumptions we have about the role of time in the evaluation and development of high-level careers. For too long it has been assumed that long hours equate with productivity, an assumption anchored in assembly-line work.

The opportunity to work part-time at senior levels can help redress the underrepresentation of women in senior and managerial positions. The current lack of women senior managers and directors is a huge waste of resources and potential, leaving the employer with a greatly reduced pool of employees from which to recruit and develop senior managers. Furthermore, some jobs of a specialist nature may not need full-time cover, particularly in smaller organisations. To quote a respondent to the Balanced Lives survey already cited, 'The Chief Executive (who I report to) said we hire you for your brains not the number of hours you sit in an office.'

An increasingly accepted way of introducing part-time working into traditionally full-time – particularly managerial – jobs is through job-sharing. For example, the retailers Boots and ASDA both offer job-share schemes at senior levels to facilitate the retention of highly skilled staff with management capability.

Work redesign

There are no immutable rules about how to structure part-time work but, in arriving at decisions, an employer has an opportunity to change existing working practices. It can provide the justification for re-evaluating what work needs to be done and for discarding work no longer of benefit to the organisation.

Where restructuring occurs in response to an employee's desire to work fewer days a week, it can provide an opportunity to reassign some of that employee's tasks, creating a larger job for someone else who may welcome more responsibility.

Restructuring a job in this way can also help recruitment for hard-to-fill vacancies. It may be that an existing employee is willing to cover the more specialist aspects of the job on a reduced-hours basis, while a new, less skilled worker can be recruited to cover the rest of the work. Where several employees wish to work reduced hours, it is often possible to 'pool' the saved days to create further part- or full-time positions.

Job-sharing and job-splitting

Job-sharing typically involves filling an established (often senior) job in a different way. Although some such jobs are in reality shared, others are split, with tasks divided between two part-time job-holders. It is not always easy to distinguish a job-share from a job-split. Indeed, they tend to form two ends of a continuum.

Where a job is shared, the parts of the job continue to be linked together and cannot be run in total separation. Both sharers are equally responsible for the whole job, and part of their role is to work together to ensure that nothing is missed or lost. A key element in sharing is the continuing joint responsibility for tasks.

The advantage of a job-share to the organisation is that

the job continues to exist in its full-time format and so a full-time employee can be moved into it at some later stage if desired. A further advantage is that there are always two people to provide cover – particularly in emergencies. Depending on the needs of the organisation, holidays can be taken at the same time or staggered, each job-share partner providing holiday cover for the other.

The biggest potential difficulty with job-sharing is finding a suitable partner. This is likely to be easier in large organisations than in small. One respondent to a TMP Worldwide survey described her possible dilemma[5]:

> Working on a job-share basis my job security is dependent on there being another job-share for the other half of the week. I wish there was another way around this, as there are problems recruiting to job-share vacancies. If no one is recruited you face the decision to be forced to work full-time or leave.

In job-splitting, two people simply divide one job between them so that both parts are covered. The work routines are fairly well established, and the need for co-ordination between them is minimal. The main rationale for job-splitting tends to be achieving flexibility of cover, labour-cost reduction or job creation. Job-splitting can be an effective way of achieving continuity of cover for longer than a standard working week without the addition of a second half-time job: for example, a full-time job can be split into two 60 per cent jobs.

An advantage of job-splitting is that the job can be split unevenly, separating the skilled elements from the lesser or unskilled elements. A more junior employee can then be recruited into the less skilled part of the job-split.

Jobs requiring continuity – in the sense that a responsible job-holder needs to be around throughout the working week to be accountable to others or to provide a continuous service to colleagues – are often seen as unsuitable for sharing or splitting. Those which are defined by output – such as specialist professional jobs, project-based jobs, and many clerical and administrative jobs – are seen as more suitable. The IES has found that job-sharing tends to be concentrated in the service sector whereas job-splitting is found both in manufacturing and services industries.

Either option can potentially increase costs. There may be a need for additional furniture and equipment, for instance, where sharers work together during a hand-over period. Training costs may also be higher.

A practical consideration with job-sharing is the time needed to formalise arrangements. The organisation needs to assess the suitability of a job for sharing, to decide how it should be divided and to recruit a job-share partner. Many employers therefore require a period of notice (say three months) when an employee makes a request to job-share. Setting up a job-share can be a complex process, and the decision to do so should not be undertaken lightly. Issues that should be considered are covered in the next two sections.

Job-share or job-split?

Although people talk about job-sharing and job-splitting, in reality it can sometimes be hard to determine into which category a particular post falls. In addition, an employer may decide to create a job-share in order to retain the job in its full-time form where a job-split would be more appropriate but would probably result in the development of two separate part-time jobs.

As a general guide, job-share is more likely when:

- a more senior post is involved
- higher levels of skill and responsibility are required
- the post-holder has a high degree of discretion over the content and organisation of the work
- there is a hand-over of tasks from one sharer to the other
- the job is being divided to retain highly skilled staff unable to work full-time.

In contrast, where there is a job-split:

- the post is likely to be more junior
- lower levels of skill and responsibility are required
- the post-holder has less autonomy and discretion over the work
- the work is likely to be more systematised
- tasks can be completed in the hours worked, with little or no requirement for a hand-over
- the purpose of the split is to create new jobs or to achieve cost reductions.

From its own research the IES has suggested that, at the two extremes, most professional and managerial jobs are job-shares, whereas divided jobs at the routine clerical or semi-/unskilled shop-floor level are almost always job-splits. However, between the two extremes fall a number of divided jobs that are harder to define – such as secretarial, junior administrative and technical work. Whether a given post is a job-share or job-split depends on the precise content of the job and how it is organised. New Ways to Work runs a telephone helpline providing advice on job-sharing and job-splitting.

How to make a job-share work

To be successful, a job-share should be planned thoroughly. In particular, the following issues need to be addressed:

- *What are the peaks and troughs of the current workload? How should the hours be arranged so that both sharers have an equal workload?* The most common job-share arrangement is for two people to work two-and-a-half or three days each, with an overlap period. A few job-sharers work alternate weeks. An uneven split, where one sharer works two days while the other works three, is also possible (if acceptable to both parties). In some jobs, tasks are carried out by whoever is there, whereas in others clients, projects or cases are allocated to each sharer.
- *What hand-over arrangements will be needed? How will the job-sharers communicate with each other?* Some arrangements allow for a period when both sharers are at work. Others communicate by telephone or write things in a book.
- *Can the sharer who is not working be contacted by telephone if necessary?* Some sharers do not wish to be contacted at home unless there is an emergency, while others are happy to resolve queries as they arise. The situation should be clarified at the outset to avoid later misunderstandings.
- *What will be the effect on pay and other benefits?* The implications for pay and benefits must be spelt out. For example, in most share arrangements overtime is paid (if at all) only when the full-time hours for the week have been worked. A sharer covering for his or her partner will therefore be paid only at the

standard rate. Where the share is being undertaken in preparation for retirement, the reduction in salary may affect pension payments under a final salary scheme.

- *How well are the sharers likely to work together?* Co-operation among job-sharers is essential; not surprisingly, therefore, many commentators agree that successful job-shares are based on mutual trust and respect. Where the two sharers already know and understand each other they are (obviously) likely to find it easier to work together than if a new sharer has been recruited from outside the organisation.

- *How will the work be assessed? How will the sharers be appraised?* Where sharers have specific responsibilities, this will be reasonably straightforward. Where both cover the entire spectrum of tasks, 360-degree feedback can produce valuable insights. Part of the appraisal should also be to consider how well the two sharers are working together, and the impact of this on colleagues, subordinates and customers. Some organisations choose to appraise sharers individually, and then arrange a joint discussion to set objectives for the coming year.

- *How will the sharers be promoted?* Promoting individual job-sharers is not always straightforward, particularly where one post-holder is perceived to be performing better than the other. Promoting one will mean finding new job-share partners for both. In addition, the post-holder not promoted might feel undervalued and overlooked. The issue of promoting job-sharers is probably easier to accommodate in larger than smaller organisations.

● *What is the likely impact of the proposed arrangement on work colleagues and third parties?* In particular, will the proposed arrangement create undue pressure on work colleagues, and will there be adequate cover and continuity for customers or clients?

Using technology to ease administration

A common concern about the introduction of part-time working is that it will increase the administrative burden placed upon the organisation. Until recently this was likely to be true, but new software packages not only reduce the burden but can also enhance management information, enabling overstretched managers to make more informed decisions about work-scheduling.

The newest packages operate in conjunction with Windows™-based technologies making them extremely user-friendly. Because they are accessible whenever a computer is switched on they are particularly useful for recording the activities of staff working unsociable (eg night-time) shifts.

Typically, a package can be used to monitor hours worked (including overtime hours) and sickness absence – with the potential to be linked directly to payroll for pay adjustments. Most packages provide standard management-reporting facilities, and the reports can be used to analyse trends over time, thus improving the planning and management of future workloads. In addition, employees can chart their own progress against agreed learning objectives and managers can review their records at convenient times.

The available systems fall into two groups: smaller, HR-

79

specific packages, normally offered with an option to integrate with payroll; and HR modules for larger, enterprise-wide systems.

HR-specific packages tend to be more popular among respondents to the IPD's regular *Computers in Personnel* survey. They are usually quicker and easier to install, and allow the product most appropriate to the needs of the business to be selected. They are more likely to be relevant for smaller businesses with fewer employees, and some can be upgraded as the business grows, although not all of them interface easily with other software.

Enterprise-wide systems are much larger, more expensive and take longer to install, with the HR module one of many covering every aspect of the organisation's processes. They tend to be easier to integrate and to upgrade. Where an organisation has made the decision to install an enterprise-wide (or ERP – Enterprise Resource Planning) system, managers are likely to find that the HR module can be harnessed to manage many aspects of reduced-hours working.

The IPD has produced a guide on implementing personnel systems, whereas Incomes Data Services (IDS) has produced a study on integrated HR and payroll software[6, 7]. A wealth of information about individual products can also be found on manufacturers' websites. The IES offers practical expert and independent advice on IT systems for the HR field.

References

1 NEW WAYS TO WORK. *Balanced Lives: Changing work patterns for men.* London, 1995.
2 HASTINGS M. *Flexibility and Fairness: A survey of managers'*

attitudes to part-time employment and part-time employees. London, Institute of Management. 1996.

3 IRS. *Employment Review.* No.632. May 1997.

4 See reference no.1 above.

5 TMP WORLDWIDE. *The Flexible Workforce – Fact or Fiction? A major survey into the realities of new working patterns.* London, 1998.

6 IPD. *The IPD Guide on Implementing Computerised Personnel Systems.* London, IPD, 1997.

7 IDS. *Integrated HR and Payroll Software.* IDS Study Plus. November 1998.

Resources list

The Association of British Chambers of Commerce
Manning House
Carlisle Place
London
SW1P 1JA
Tel: 020-7565 2000

Can provide details of your local chamber of commerce.

The Carers National Association
20–25 Glasshouse Yard
London
EC1A 4JS
Tel: 020-7490 8818

The Carers National Association campaigns for better services and changes in legislation which will help carers to combine employment with their caring duties. The Association also advises employers on their policies and practice.

The Carers in Employment Group
c/o The Princess Royal Trust for Carers
16 Byward Street
London
EC3R 5BA
Tel: 020-7480 7788

The Princess Royal Trust for Carers offers information, advice and support to carers through its nationwide network of Carers Centres.

Employers' Forum on Age
Astral House
1268 London Road
London
SW16 4ER
Tel: 020-8765 7280

The Employers' Forum on Age provides a one-stop shop for information and guidance on deriving business advantage from a mixed-age workforce.

Employers' Forum on Disability
Nutmeg House
60 Gainsford Street
London
SE1 2NY
Tel: 020-7403 3020
Fax: 020-7403 0404

This is the national forum for employers wishing to develop and establish good practice in relation to employing disabled people and serving them as customers. It has an information line and a range of publications.

The Equal Opportunities Commission (EOC)
Overseas House
Quay Street
Manchester
M3 3HN
Tel: 0161-833 9244

Runs the Equality Exchange, a network for employers, trainers and consultants. Benefits of being a network member include bi-monthly mailings on all the latest developments in gender equality, expert advice on issues relating to promoting equal opportunities at work, information packs and guidance notes on best practice, seminars and conferences and access to research reports.

The Industrial Society
Peter Runge House
3 Carlton House Terrace
London
SW1Y 5DG
Tel: 020-7479 1000
Fax: 020-7479 2222

An independent, non-profit campaigning body with over 10,000 member organisations from every part of the economy. The Society runs training courses and conferences, provides advice (including an employment law helpline) and consultancy services, and publishes books, reports and video training packages.

The Institute for Employment Studies (IES)

Mantell Building
University of Sussex
Brighton
BN1 9RF
Tel: 01273-686 751
Fax: 01273-690 430

The IES is an independent international centre of research and consultancy in HR issues. Since it was established 25 years ago the Institute has been a focus of knowledge and practical experience in employment and training policy, the operation of labour markets and HR planning and development. Formerly titled the Institute of Manpower Studies, the organisation was renamed in 1994 to better reflect the full range of its activities and involvement.

The Institute of Personnel and Development (IPD)

IPD House
Camp Road
Wimbledon
SW19 4UX
Tel: 020-8971 9000
Fax: 020-8263 3333

Formed in 1994 from the Institute of Personnel Management and the Institute of Training and Development, the IPD has almost 100,000 members and is the professional institute of those involved in the management and development of people. It provides an extremely wide range of services to benefit individuals, employers and the wider community: training courses, consultancy services, library and information services, legal advice, publications on all HR topics, and of course professional qualifications.

New Ways to Work
309 Upper Street
London
N1 2TY
Tel/Fax: 020-7354 2978
Help ine 020-7226 4026

Aims to change the culture of the workplace to give real freedom of choice to individuals who cannot or do not wish to work traditional work patterns. Through education and research it aims to advance knowledge about all aspects of flexible work patterns.

Parents at Work
5th Floor
45 Beech Street
London
EC2Y 8AD
Tel: 020-7628 3565

Parents at Work is a campaigning charity with both individual parent and corporate members. It has been promoting the business case for family-friendly working since the
mid-1980s. Services to corporates include seminars, net-
working events, member-to-member support, the annual
Employer of the Year Award and work–home balance consultancy.

The Qualifications and Curriculum Authority
29 Bolton Street
London
W1Y 7PD
Tel: 020-7509 5555

Can provide details of relevant NVQs and awarding bodies
for your industry.

Roffey Park Management Institute
Forest Road
Horsham
West Sussex
RH12 4TD
Tel: 01293-851 644
Fax: 01293-851 565

Roffey Park's areas of expertise include organisational and
management development at all levels, managing change,
training developers and interpersonal skills development.
These are delivered through short residential programmes,
in-company development and consultancy, all under-

pinned by extensive research into such areas as flexible and part-time working, mergers and acquisitions and work–life balance. Information can be accessed through seminars, workshops, publications and reports.

The TEC National Council

Westminster Tower
Albert Embankment
London
SE1 7SX
Tel: 020-7735 0010

Can provide details of your local Training and Enterprise Council (TEC).

The Women Returners' Network (WRN)

344-354 Gray's Inn Road
London
WC1X 8BP
Answerphone/Helpline 020-7278 2900
Fax: 020-7278 2722

WRN was founded in 1984 and seeks to facilitate the re-entry of women into education, training and employment. It now has over 300 members nationally, a telephone helpline, an information database of all important issues for women's education, training and employment, and regional directories of education and training.

Bibliography

CAMPBELL N. J. *Writing Effective Policies and Procedures.* American Management Association, 1997.

HAMMOND SUDDARDS. *Disability Discrimination.* London, IPD, 1999.

PALMER C., MOON G. *and* COX S. *Discrimination at Work.* 3rd edn. Legal Action Group, 1997.

PARENTS AT WORK. *Tomorrow's Companies Today: Success stories from the Employer of the Year Awards.* London, 1999.

STREDWICK J. *and* ELLIS S. *Flexible Working Practices: Techniques and innovations.* London, IPD, 1998.

Appendix: Suggested draft policy

As we have said in section 3 ('How do I create a policy for part-time workers?'), every employer's policy is likely to be different. The policy should accommodate the needs of your business and sit comfortably alongside your other policies. The example below is one suggestion for a draft policy. In addition, it is recommended that you provide a standard *pro forma* form for applicants to complete when applying for reduced hours. This should include proposed changes to hours, flexible work options or recommendations for work re-organisation. It should also demonstrate how the needs of the organisation have been taken into account in their proposal and any potential benefits as a result of the change.

Reduced Hours (Part-Time) Working Policy

As an employer we are happy to consider innovative ways to organise work and welcome ideas that benefit the organisation in terms of meeting operational needs and enhancing staff recruitment or retention. We value diversity and are striving to create a flexible working environment that takes into account individuals' needs alongside other members of staff and the requirements of the job.

Should your circumstances require a reduction in working hours, either short-term or permanently, we will try to accommodate your needs, and can discuss a range of flexible working options. All members of staff are eligible to apply but each case will be considered on its merits, taking into account the needs of the job, current work performance and other factors as laid out below.

1 The option to work reduced hours is available at all grades, including senior management.

2. When filling a new vacancy, managers are encouraged to consider alternative working arrangements where appropriate and feasible.

3 Requests from current employees for a change in their hours of work should be made at least one month prior to the date on which they wish to work the new hours. Employees will not normally be allowed to change their hours of work more frequently than at six-monthly intervals.

4 Maintenance of operational standards is important to the success of the organisation and all requests for reduced hours working must be considered in this context. It will help your application if there is a clear business-based justification for altering your hours.

5 All requests will be dealt with through a fair and consistent process to ensure equal treatment.

6 Practical considerations, such as which flexible option would best suit the needs of the individual and the job,

should be discussed at an early stage. The impact on customers, colleagues and performance should also be considered and will be a key factor in reaching a final decision. HR can advise on the most appropriate reduced hours arrangements for a specific function.

7 Current job performance will be taken into account in all applications.

8 Initially, you should discuss your application with your line manager who will consult with personnel. The decision to allow or refuse a reduced hours arrangement rests with the Personnel Manager and will be made within two weeks of the request being submitted. Employees who are unsatisfied with the Personnel Manager's decision may appeal under the appeals procedure set out in the staff handbook. Appeals will be heard by the Finance Director, whose decision will be final.

9 Reasons for a refusal will be held on file in personnel and applicants may submit another application after six months when circumstances may have changed.

10 Once an application has been approved, a start date will be agreed and there will be a review after three months to ensure the new arrangement is working both for the individual, their manager and any other team members.

11 We recognise the valuable contribution made to our organisation by those who work reduced hours and will treat them equally with full-time staff. Reduced hours workers will be entitled to all statutory and contractual benefits on a *pro-rata* basis.